JENNIFER
LAWRENCE

By Marie Morreale

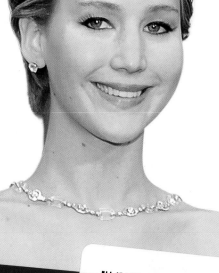

Children's Press
An Imprint of Scholastic Inc.
New York   Toronto   London   Auckland   Sydney
Mexico City   New Delhi   Hong Kong
Danbury, Connecticut

D1295189

Photos ©: Alamy Images: 22 top (AF archive), 39 center right (Mediablitzimages), 27 (Moviestore collection Ltd), 22 bottom (Photos 12), 24 top (Pictorial Press Ltd), 31 (Zuma Press, Inc.); AP Images: 18, 23 (Chris Pizzello/Invision), 38 bottom (Dave Bedrosian/Geisler-Fotopress/picture-alliance/dpa), 28 (Evan Agostini/Invision), 26 (Jordan Strauss/Invision); Dreamstime: 15 bottom (Christopher Elwell), 13 bottom left (Kateleigh), 41 bottom (Sbukley); Everett Collection: 14 right (Derek Storm), 21 bottom (TBS), 15 top left; Getty Images: 44 (Anthony Harvey), 9 (CBS Photo Archive), 36, 37 (Gerard McGovern), 40 center (Graham Denholm), 32 (Gregg DeGuire), back cover (Jason Merritt), 16 (Jason Squires), 34 (Jesse Grant), cover, 4 - 5 (Juan Naharro Gimenez), 1 (Kevin Mazur), 7 (Kevin Winter), 21 top (Murray Close), 25 bottom, 42 top right (NBC), 12 right (Ray Tamarra), 2, 3 (Venturelli); Kobal Collection/Atlas Entertainment: 26; Landov/Lucas Jackson/Reuters: 6; Newscom: 8 (AP1 Wenn Photos), 35 (CB2/ZOB/Supplied by WENN.com), 29 (Paul Andrews, CelebrityHomePhotos); Rex USA : 11; Seth Poppel Yearbook Library: 13 top; Shutterstock, Inc.: 15 top right (Adisa), 38 - 43 background (conejota), 12 left, 14 left (CrackerClips Stock Media), 13 bottom right (Csanad Kiss), 39 top right (Featureflash), 13 center, 40 bottom, 41 top, 41 center (Helga Esteb), 43 bottom right (LunaseeStudios), 43 center left (Mariontxa), 39 top center, 42 bottom left, 42 center right (My Life Graphic), 38 top, 39 center left, 40 top, 43 bottom left (Nonnakrit), 43 (Roman Samokhin), 39 top left, 42 top left and bottom right, 43 top (seregam), 39 bottom (VladislavGudovskiy).

Library of Congress Cataloging-in-Publication Data
Morreale, Marie.
  Jennifer Lawrence / by Marie Morreale.
    pages cm. — (Real bios)
  Includes bibliographical references and index.
  ISBN 978-0-531-21375-9 (library binding) —
ISBN 978-0-531-21428-2 (pbk.)
1. Lawrence, Jennifer, 1990– —Juvenile literature. 2. Actors—United States—Biography—Juvenile literature. I. Title.
PN2287.L28948M68 2015
791.4302'8092—dc23[B]   2014031106

1 2 3 4 5 6 7 8 9 10 R 24 23 22 21 20 19 18 17 16 15

Jennifer is red-carpet perfection at the 86th Annual Academy Awards!

MEET JENNIFER!
GIRL ON THE MOVE!

Jennifer Lawrence has appeared in dozens of films, won an Oscar and multiple other awards, and become a kid icon for her roles as Katniss Everdeen in the *Hunger Games* series and Mystique in the *X-Men* series. All this and she's not even 25 years old! And best of all, she's really funny. Jennifer would rather be out climbing hills or riding horses than going to a Hollywood event and facing the flashes of the **paparazzi**. Believe it or not, she even claims she is boring! Once you've read this *Real Bio*, you'll see that this isn't true. Jennifer is absolutely amazing!

CONTENTS

Jennifer sizzled at the premiere of *The Hunger Games: Catching Fire.*

JENNIFER LAWRENCE:
A STAR IS BORN

FROM TOMBOY TO TEEN STAR

Gary and Karen Lawrence had a comfortable life back in 1990. They had two sons, Ben and Blaine. The family lived on a small horse farm in Indian Hills, a suburb of Louisville, Kentucky. Gary ran a successful concrete business, and Karen ran Camp Hi Ho, a summer camp for kids. Then, on August 15, 1990, Gary and Karen's third child, Jennifer, was born. Things were never the same in the Lawrence household!

From the beginning, it was obvious that Jennifer, nicknamed Jenny Lou, was full of energy. Even as a toddler, she ran instead of walked. She preferred playing sports and riding horses to Barbie dolls. She simply wasn't girlie-girlie. One word described her— tomboy. Of course, having two older brothers helped

(Opposite page) Jennifer and her family are joyous over her Oscar win for *Silver Linings Playbook*. (Left) Jennifer is picture perfect as she accepts her award.

"I HAVE AN OVERACTIVE IMAGINATION. I STILL HAVE THE MIND OF AN 11-YEAR-OLD."

shape her personality. There were no afternoon tea parties with her dolls. No dress-up and makeup sessions. The Lawrence siblings showed their affection a bit differently. "My brothers and I would scream at each other, and we'd be like, 'I hate you! You're so stupid! You're ugly!'" she told *InStyle* magazine. "And then five minutes later it would be, 'I love you.'"

"I NEVER PLAY CHARACTERS THAT ARE LIKE ME BECAUSE I'M A BORING PERSON."

The Lawrence household was definitely rough-and-tumble, but it was surrounded with lots of love. Most kids who have brothers or sisters can probably relate. "Being the youngest and the only girl, I think everyone

Jennifer waves to the paparazzi lining the red carpet at the Venice Film Festival.

It's always a laugh riot when Jennifer appears on *The Late Show with David Letterman*.

was so worried about me being a brat that they went in the exact opposite direction of treating me like Cinderella," she laughingly told *Elle* magazine.

Jennifer loved her early childhood. She was a nature lover who rode her favorite pony, Muffin, as she explored the woods on the family farm. She also asked questions constantly. She was full of life. "My nickname was 'Nitro' as [in] nitroglycerin," Jennifer explained to *Madame Figaro* magazine. "I was hyperactive, curious about everything. When my mother told me about my childhood, she always told me there was like a light in me, a spark that inspired me constantly. When I entered the school, the light went out. We never knew what it was, a kind of social **anxiety**."

"I didn't want her to be a diva," Karen Lawrence told *Rolling Stone* magazine. "I didn't mind if she was girlie, as long as she was tough." Unfortunately, Jennifer was a little too tough for preschool—the teachers wouldn't let her play with the other little girls. "She didn't mean to hurt them," Karen explained. "They were just making cookies, and she wanted to play ball."

Even though Jennifer was tough, she was targeted by bullies. As a result, school was not her favorite place. She remembers that she spent a lot of time crying during the school year. "I changed schools a lot when I was in elementary school because some girls were mean," Jennifer told *The Sun* newspaper. "They were less mean in middle school, because I was doing all right, although this one girl gave me invitations to hand out to her birthday party that I wasn't invited to. But that was fine. I just hocked a loogie on them and threw them in the trash."

Even though things got a bit better as school went on, Jennifer still had to deal with this strange insecurity she had. "I was a weirdo," Jennifer explained to *Vogue* magazine. ". . . I wasn't smarter than the other

Katniss Barbie

A collector's edition of the doll was based on her *Hunger Games* character.

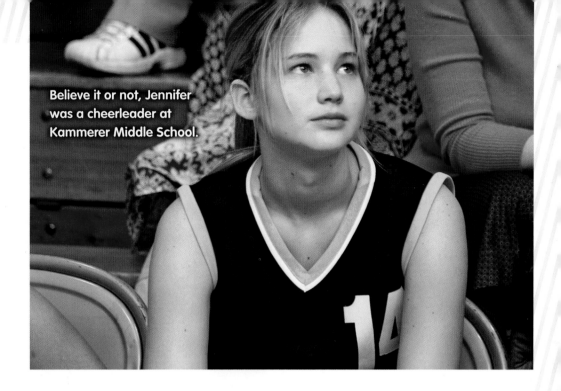

Believe it or not, Jennifer was a cheerleader at Kammerer Middle School.

kids; that's not why I didn't fit in. I've always just had this weird anxiety. I hated recess. I didn't like field trips. Parties really stressed me out. And I had a very different sense of humor. . . . My family went on a cruise, and I got a terrible haircut. FYI: Never get your hair cut on a cruise. And I had, like, this blonde curly 'fro, and I walked into the gym the first day back in seventh grade and everyone was staring at me, and for some reason I thought, I know what I need to do! And I just started sprinting from one end of the gym to the other, and I thought it was hilarious. But nobody else at that age really did. It was genuinely weird."

In spite of her anxiety, Jennifer tried to fit in. She explored activities that she thought she might be good at. At the age of nine, she was in a church play based on the book of Jonah. She liked it so much that she started appearing in both school musicals and more church plays. The little girl who stressed out about going to parties shined like a star onstage in front of hundreds of people!

While still in middle school, Jennifer decided that acting was her future. She recalled the moment in an interview with *Glamour* magazine. "I read a script. I wasn't the best student. I got A's and B's, but I remember being in the classroom

FACT FILE

THE BASICS

Jennifer Strong

"I like when things are hard; I'm very competitive."

FULL NAME: Jennifer Shrader Lawrence

NICKNAMES: Nitro, Jenny Lou, J-Law

BIRTHDAY: August 15, 1990

BIRTHPLACE: Louisville, Kentucky

HERITAGE: English, German, Irish, and Scottish

CURRENT HOME: Los Angeles, California

SCHOOLS: Kammerer Middle School and High School

MIDDLE SCHOOL HONOR: Voted "Most Talkative"

MIDDLE SCHOOL EXTRACURRICULAR: Cheerleading

SUMMER JOB: Assistant to the nurse at her mom's Camp Hi Ho

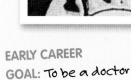

EARLY CAREER GOAL: To be a doctor

CURRENT PETS: A cat named Cleo and a Labrador retriever named Spinee

CAREER ROLE MODELS: Meryl Streep, Jodie Foster

CELEBRITY CRUSHES: John Stamos, Daniel Radcliffe, 'N Sync

MUSICAL INSTRUMENT: Guitar

BEST FRIEND: Her assistant, Justine

HOBBIES: Painting, knitting

CHILDHOOD PETS: Four ponies named Muffin, Dan, Brumby, and Brandy; three dachshunds; a cat named Shadow

and looking around and being like, 'Oh, all of you get this' and just feeling stupid. And then I read a script, and I just fell in love. I didn't feel stupid anymore. I just found something I was good at."

Jennifer announced her goal as soon as she got home. She also decided that she had to move to New York City to become a true actress. So Jennifer did her best to convince her parents that they should go to the Big Apple. Finally Karen gave in. When Jennifer was 14, she and her mom went to New York City for spring break. Karen considered it

FACT FILE

FAVORITES

Dr. Lawrence
"I wanted to be a doctor when I was little, so I'm okay with blood and guts."

MOVIES: The Big Lebowski, Harold and Maude, Midnight in Paris

TV SERIES: Full House

MUSIC VIDEO: "I'm a Slave 4 U" by Britney Spears

CANDY: Baby Ruth, Laffy Taffy

NUTS: Almonds

CAKE: Funfetti, with vanilla or strawberry icing

BREAKFAST: Scrambled eggs and bacon

DINNER: Baby back ribs, spaghetti Bolognese

FAST FOOD: French fries, pizza, cheesesteak subs

SPORTS: Horseback riding, basketball, field hockey, and softball

CAR: Her old VW Eos

HEELS OR FLATS: FLATS! "I'm terrible in heels . . . I can't walk, and my feet are uncomfortable."

a vacation, but Jennifer hoped that it would be her big break. Guess what . . . Jennifer was right!

One day Jennifer and her mom were exploring the city's downtown area when they stopped to watch some break-dancers. Suddenly, a talent scout approached them and asked if Jennifer would be interested in working as a model! When Jennifer and Karen returned home, they discussed it with the entire family. Karen and Gary were skeptical, but Jennifer was very persuasive. She finally convinced her parents to let her return to New York during the summer. Her brother Blaine went with her. They found an apartment in Manhattan. Jennifer got an agent and booked several commercials and some modeling jobs.

Jennifer is the first to tell you she's most comfortable in a t-shirt and jeans.

But after about six weeks, Jennifer's dad went to New York to bring his children home. Just as they were about to return to Kentucky, Jennifer landed a role on a TV **pilot**. Her father was still determined to bring Jennifer home. Ben and Blaine intervened, though. Jennifer told *Elle*, "My brothers called [my parents] and said, 'She's been to every football game. She's been to every baseball game. This is her baseball diamond—you guys would do it if it were the World Series. You guys have to do it for her.'"

Karen and Gary finally agreed to let Jennifer keep working, but they set some basic rules. Jennifer had to finish high school online. Also, whenever she had to go to New York or Los Angeles for an **audition** or job, one of her parents had to go with her. Soon, Jennifer won small roles in TV series such as *Cold Case* and *Monk*. Just as she turned 17, she landed the role of Lauren Pearson on the TBS comedy *The Bill Engvall Show*. The show lasted three seasons. During that time, Jennifer won the Young Artist Award for Outstanding Young Performer in a TV Series. Little did she know that it wouldn't be the last time she walked onstage to accept an award!

> "MY PARENTS ALWAYS HAD TO TELL ME STORIES, OR I WAS TELLING STORIES, READING STORIES."

Another award for Jennifer's collection—the Independent Spirit Award for *Silver Linings Playbook*.

CATCHING FIRE!

AWKWARD TEEN TO ROLE MODEL

TV series and commercials helped pay the rent, but Jennifer was dreaming of a big-screen role. Movies—that's what acting was all about. She landed her first major film audition in 2007. She was up for the role of Bella Swan in the *Twilight* franchise. Another newcomer, Kristen Stewart, eventually got the role, but the experience just made Jennifer hungrier for the right script.

By 2008, Jennifer was making a name for herself in small independent films. Her big break came in 2010, when she was cast in *Winter's Bone*. The movie was a dark murder mystery. Jennifer played the tough 17-year-old Ree Dolly, who had to raise her younger brother and sister by herself. She awed critics and audiences with her in-your-face take on this squirrel-cooking, wood-chopping mountain girl. As a matter of fact, she impressed the film industry so much that she was nominated for a Best Actress award at the Oscars, a Critics' Choice Movie Award, and a Screen Actors

Yum Yum! Jennifer ate a Philly cheesesteak right before she went to the 2011 Oscars.

Guild Award. She wasn't even upset that she lost the Best Actress Oscar to Natalie Portman for *Black Swan*. She was honored just to be nominated!

Now that Jennifer was making a name for herself, she was offered bigger and bigger roles. In 2011, she took on the role of Mystique in *X-Men: First Class*. She was thrilled to finally play a totally different type of character. "It's easy to get pigeonholed, so I think it's important that when one thing gets really big—it's a wise decision to do the opposite," she told *TeenVogue* magazine.

Starring in a big-budget film is very different from acting in an independent movie. For one thing, there are definitely more comforts given to the stars of major films like *X-Men: First Class*. "I had a blast," Jennifer continued with *TeenVogue*. "I was living in London for five months, and the whole cast . . . we all legitimately love each other. We got addicted to hanging out."

One of her fellow cast members, Nicholas Hoult (who

Jennifer's Timeline

JOURNEY OF SUCCESS

SEPTEMBER 2007
Jennifer costars in the TBS series *The Bill Engvall Show*.

2008
Jennifer has roles in the films *Poker House* and *The Burning Plain*.

MAY 30, 2008
Jennifer's first movie, *Garden Party*, is released—she has a small role.

Playing Mystique in *X-Men* movie series was awesome for Jennifer!

played Beast), even became her boyfriend! But the things she remembers most about the role of Mystique are the training and the makeup. It wasn't easy to get into Mystique shape. "It was two hours [a day] of weight training and circuits," Jennifer told *People* magazine. "She's a superhero, and I'm a wimp, so I had to get some muscle." And for the character's blue skin,

MARCH 29, 2009
Jennifer wins Outstanding Young Performer in a TV Series for *The Bill Engvall Show* at the Young Artist Awards.

Jennifer loves the strength of Katniss Everdeen in the *Hunger Games* movies.

Jennifer needed "a few layers of airbrushed body paint, five layers of splattered paint and strategically placed scales. The entire process took about eight to ten hours."

Needless to say, after *X-Men: First Class*, the scripts came flying in to Jennifer's agent. Everyone wanted Jennifer Lawrence in their movies! But it was Karen who unknowingly guided her toward the right films. "My mom's just developed this brand new reputation of being a complete stage mom because the two books she's ever

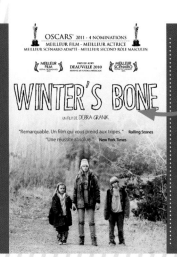

JUNE 11, 2010
Winter's Bone is released.

2011
Jennifer has roles in the films *Like Crazy* and *The Beaver*.

FEBRUARY 27, 2011
Jennifer is nominated for Best Actress for *Winter's Bone* at the 83rd Academy Awards.

JUNE 3, 2011
X-Men: First Class hits theaters.

recommended I read have been *Winter's Bone* and *The Hunger Games*, without any idea that they would ever be movies," Jennifer revealed to denofgeek.com. "She gave me her books."

When Jennifer found out that *The Hunger Games* was being made into a movie series, she knew right away she wanted to be part of it. The role of Katniss Everdeen was sought after by many young stars in Hollywood. But Jennifer nailed her audition with the film's director Gary Ross. "I'd never seen an audition that good. Ever," Ross told MTV News. "I saw someone who I knew was going to be working for decades."

Jennifer was happy and scared at the same time when she learned that she had won the role of Katniss. She knew it would mean months of preparation, including

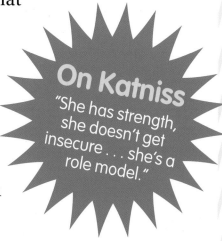

On Katniss
"She has strength, she doesn't get insecure . . . she's a role model."

MARCH 23, 2012
The Hunger Games is released.

JUNE 3, 2012
Wins MTV Movie award for Best Female Performance for *The Hunger Games*.

JULY 22, 2012
Jennifer wins Teen Choice Awards for Choice Sci-Fi/Fantasy Actress, Choice Liplock, and Choice Best Chemistry for *The Hunger Games*.

Jennifer and Liam Hemsworth (Gale) became great friends while making *The Hunger Games.*

learning archery, building up her body, and even doing yoga so she "could be catlike." But she also felt a sense of responsibility. "I love Katniss," she told *Parade* magazine. "She doesn't have a lot, but she's happy, and she faces death out of love for her family. She doesn't want to be a hero, but she becomes a symbol for a revolution, a kind of futuristic Joan of Arc."

SEPTEMBER 21, 2012
Jennifer's film *House at the End of the Street* hits theaters.

DECEMBER 25, 2012
Silver Linings Playbook is released.

JANUARY 13, 2013
Jennifer wins Best Actress—Motion Picture for *Silver Linings Playbook* at the Golden Globe Awards.

JANUARY 19, 2013
Jennifer hosts *Saturday Night Live.*

Jennifer had experienced some of the Hollywood hype with *X-Men: First Class*, but she wasn't prepared for the hysteria over *The Hunger Games*. The most popular book series since *Harry Potter* had a built-in audience. That was something Jennifer learned pretty quickly. "The day the first *Hunger Games* came out was a kind of bizarre day for me because I wasn't famous 24 hours earlier and I got up to go about my day as usual and went to the grocery store," she told *The Telegraph* newspaper. "All of a sudden there were like 25 paparazzi following me and there was a three-car pileup. I was really terrified and I went home and locked myself in the house. I couldn't really process anything. Then my doorbell rang and all of my friends were there with [goodies]. They came in and we all just kind of

Friendship

Jennifer and *HG* costars Josh Hutcherson and Liam Hemsworth are BFFs.

FEBRUARY 24, 2013
Jennifer wins Best Actress for *Silver Linings Playbook* at the 85th Academy Awards.

APRIL 14, 2013
Jennifer wins MTV Movie Awards for Best Female Performance and Best Kiss for *Silver Linings Playbook*.

NOVEMBER 22, 2013
The Hunger Games: Catching Fire is released.

DECEMBER 20, 2013
American Hustle is released.

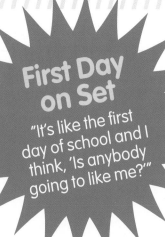

First Day on Set

"It's like the first day of school and I think, 'Is anybody going to like me?'"

watched TV and had a normal day, so that was nice."

Jennifer had little time to go back to a normal life. In 2012, she came out with two more films, *House at the End of the Street* and *Silver Linings Playbook*. Then she started seeing her face on the covers of magazines such as *Vogue*, *Vanity Fair*, *Elle*, *Glamour*, and many, many more. She became a sought-after nighttime talk show guest, visiting David Letterman, Jimmy Kimmel, and Jimmy Fallon often. The comedians knew that when Jennifer showed up, their shows would be fun and a little unpredictable.

By 2013, Jennifer was working on a number of other films—*The Devil You Know*, *The Hunger Games: Catching Fire*, and *American Hustle*. Then the most amazing thing

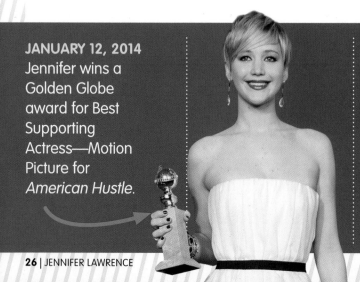

JANUARY 12, 2014
Jennifer wins a Golden Globe award for Best Supporting Actress—Motion Picture for *American Hustle*.

MARCH 2, 2014
Jennifer is nominated for Best Supporting Actress for *American Hustle* at the 86th Academy Awards.

happened to her—she won the Best Actress Oscar for *Silver Linings Playbook*! Talk about a whirlwind. Of course, Jennifer being Jennifer, she tripped on her dress and fell as she walked up the

Jennifer and *Silver Linings Playbook* costar Bradley Cooper won praise for the film.

steps to accept her award. Luckily, Jennifer has always been able to laugh at herself, and she earned a standing ovation for her speech. To top it all off, the Oscar was just one of many awards she won for her *Silver Linings Playbook* performance!

Nonstop work and back-to-back ceremonies and appearances began to take their toll on Jennifer. When

APRIL 13, 2014
Jennifer wins an MTV Movie Award for Best Female Performance for *The Hunger Games: Catching Fire*.

MAY 23, 2014
X-Men: Days of Future Past is released.

NOVEMBER 21, 2014
The Hunger Games: Mockingjay—Part 1 is released.

NOVEMBER 20, 2015
The Hunger Games: Mockingjay—Part 2 is released.

DECEMBER 25, 2015
Joy is released.

The *American Hustle* cast: (l to r) Amy Adams, Christian Bale, Jennifer Lawrence, Bradley Cooper, and Jeremy Renner.

"I'VE NEVER CRIED OVER NOT GETTING A ROLE."

she ran into *The Hunger Games* director Gary Ross at an event, he congratulated her on her success. "He was asking me what the experience was like," she told MTV News, "and I just kind of opened up and said, 'I feel like a rag doll. I have hair and makeup people coming to my house every day and putting me in new, uncomfortable, weird dresses and expensive shoes, and I just shut down and raise my arms up for them to get the dress on, and pout my lips when they need to put the lipstick on.' And we both started laughing because that's exactly what it's like for Katniss in the Capitol. She was a girl who's all of a sudden introduced to fame. I know what that feels like to have all this flurry around you and feel like, 'Oh, no, I don't belong here.'"

All of Hollywood disagreed with her on that point! Jennifer most definitely belonged there. And if she still didn't believe it then, she had to know it was true by the time she started winning awards for her *American Hustle* performance.

The year 2014 was another big one for Jennifer. She had roles in movies such as *X-Men: Days of Future Past*, *Serena*, *Dumb and Dumber To*, and *The Hunger Games: Mockingjay—Part 1*. And scheduled for 2015 were *The Hunger Games: Mockingjay—Part 2* and *Joy*.

No one would ever claim that Jennifer has let her fame and fortune go to her head. In 2014, she was still living in the same two-bedroom condo in Santa Monica, California, that she first moved into with her mom when they came out to Hollywood. She loves it and has said she doesn't need a mansion in Beverly Hills!

Her close friends have been with her for years. She shrugs off people who try to get to know her because she's famous. "I just get allergic to that kind of thing," she told *USA Today*. "People treating

Jennifer's comfy little Santa Monica house. She's happy there.

you differently when you don't feel any differently is really alienating. You can see the way they look at you. I can see if that was who I surrounded myself with, that's why you change. I find people who don't change. That's where I get my reality."

Change for Jennifer came in many ways, but one show-biz adjustment that still gets her angry is constantly being told she should be skinny. The first time she came up against that attitude has stayed with her. "I was young," she told *Bazaar* magazine. "It was just the kind of [stuff] that actresses have to go through. Somebody told me I was fat, that I was going to get fired if I didn't lose a certain amount of weight. . . . [Someone

> "THE OTHER DAY I HAD PIZZA FOR BREAKFAST, BUFFALO WINGS FOR LUNCH, AND PIZZA FOR DINNER."

brought it up recently.] They thought that because of the way my career had gone, it wouldn't still hurt me. That somehow, after I won an Oscar, I'm above it all. 'You really still care about that?' Yeah, I was a little girl. I was hurt. It doesn't matter what **accolades** you get."

Though that experience was difficult for Jennifer, it made her realize that she was happy with who she was. She has never gone through crazy dieting to get a role. As a matter of fact, she told *People*, "I don't diet. I do exercise! But I don't diet. You can't work when you're hungry, you know."

Jennifer's best advice is to keep it real. "I'm just so sick of these young girls with diets," she told *Seventeen*. "I remember when I was 13 and it was cool to pretend to have an eating disorder because there were rumors that Lindsay Lohan and Nicole Richie were anorexic. I thought it was crazy. I went home and told my mom, 'Nobody's eating bread—I just had to finish everyone's burgers.'"

And that's why everyone loves Jennifer Lawrence!

The fans and paparazzi go gaga over Jennifer!

Jennifer has the red carpet pose down pat!

THE REAL JENNIFER
LAWRENCE

THE HUNGER GAMES, PAPARAZZI, BIG EGOS & MORE!

Jennifer has always been known to speak her mind. If you ask her a question, she will tell you exactly what she thinks. Sometimes it's funny; sometimes it's outrageous. No matter what, it's always pure Jennifer!

On her favorite quality of *The Hunger Games*'s Katniss Everdeen . . . "Katniss is focused on her survival and a revolution, not who is going to be her boyfriend. Hopefully these movies will make young girls feel more powerful, which is the goal."

On actors who have big egos . . . "I just don't get it. I don't feel any cooler for what I do. When I meet somebody who actually does something to help other people, like a doctor or, I don't know, even a financial advisor, that's impressive to me. 'You can do math? That's amazing.'"

Jennifer and costars Liam Hemsworth and Josh Hutcherson sign autographs on the *Hunger Games* mall tour!

On her favorite day of filming *The Hunger Games* . . . "We were shooting on this beautiful beach, and there were sea turtles everywhere. In between takes Josh and Sam and I were running and jumping and swimming in the water. I was like, 'I'm getting paid to do this? This is awesome.'"

On her friendships . . . "I don't trust a girl who doesn't have any girlfriends. I have really close girlfriends, but they're guys like me—girls who eat and don't know anything about fashion."

On learning to dance for *Silver Linings Playbook* . . . "I'm a terrible dancer! It was so stressful because Bradley [Cooper] was really great. It became more and more of a stressful thing, but it was fun—like, once you actually learn a dance, it's really fun to do."

On how growing up with older brothers helped her with the role of Katniss . . . "I don't know. I get asked that question, and I think, well, running through the woods being chased by somebody with a knife, and me running through the house because my brother has a slingshot, like, I mean, they're different! Growing up with brothers has obviously shaped me, your family shapes you, but you don't really have a reference of how you would be differently."

On being candid . . . "I'm not like, 'I'm a rebel; I'm out of control.' I just don't think about things before I say them or " do them."

On the media being snarky about certain people . . . "Why is humiliating people funny? . . . I get it, and,

The Katniss Everdeen doll is pretty realistic! Jennifer loves it!

and I do it too, we all do it. [But] the media needs to take responsibility for the effect that it has on our younger generation, on these girls who are watching these television shows, and picking up how to talk and how to be cool. I mean, if we're regulating [certain things] because of the effect they have on our younger generation, why aren't we regulating things like calling people fat? . . . I just think it should be illegal to call somebody fat on TV."

Jennifer traded in her Katniss-wear for a gorgeous Oscar-ready gown!

On red carpets . . . "Red carpets are so scary. I end up getting so nervous that I get hyper. So I go into interviews and I'm like, 'I'm like a Chihuahua! I'm shaking and peeing!' And then afterward, I'm like, 'I just talked about peeing on the red carpet!'"

On flying first class . . . "I always feel like an idiot every time I fly first class because I'm a kid. And I just sit there, and everyone's got their newspapers and they're on the computer, and I'm like, 'Can I get a coloring book, please? Can I get some crayons?'"

On being a known crackup . . . "That's not because I'm funny. I'm just really immature, and I can't be serious for long or it kills me. Especially if we're doing an emotional scene—I just can't be serious."

On dieting . . . "I like food. I don't really diet or anything. I'm miserable when I'm dieting and I like the way I look. I'm really sick of all these actresses looking like birds."

JENNIFER, AT A GLANCE

A BULLETIN BOARD OF LAUGHS!

True-Blue
Family and friends are always first in Jennifer's heart of hearts!

TEEN TIMES

FIRST BOY BAND CRUSH

"My teen crush [was Justin Timberlake]. Early '90s Justin Timberlake, though. Like 'N Sync Justin Timberlake. I remember buying the 'N Sync CD. Remember how CDs had like the pullout picture things? I was like getting so overwhelmed . . . I almost threw up!"

BY THE NUMBERS

$2.79
The cost of the McDonald's Happy Meal Jennifer ate before hitting the red carpet at the 2014 Oscars.

$10,000,000
Jennifer's reported salary for starring in the *Hunger Games* sequels.

$100.00
The cost to ship a large bag of Jennifer's favorite coffee beans from Hawaii to Los Angeles.

STARSTRUCK

Though Jennifer is one of Hollywood's biggest stars, she still gets all nervous and awkward when she sees or meets one of her personal favorites. Sometimes she even loses it for not-so-famous actors. For example, she admitted, "There's a commercial for [Six Flags], and it's this old man who dances in glasses, and I thought I saw him . . . I almost had a heart attack!"

So what happens when Jennifer meets a really major star? Well, check it out . . .

Bill Clinton: One of Jennifer's most historic mistakes was when she introduced former president Bill Clinton as he received the Advocate for Change Award in 2013. "I [called] Bill Clinton 'Gill Clinton' while I was presenting him."

Brad Pitt and Angelina Jolie: Jennifer almost lost her cool at the 2014 Oscars. "Brad Pitt and Angelina Jolie were, like, two feet away from my table. And it changes you. Like, I have heart palpitations. They should be king and queen of America. I would pay taxes to them and not even think twice about it."

Jeff Bridges: At an industry event, Jennifer saw Jeff Bridges (*The Giver*) surrounded by photographers and press. At first she ran away, but when she approached him, she hugged him and said, "I'm like your biggest fan, I'm so sorry. I'm so sorry for interrupting you, there's cameras everywhere."

Daniel Radcliffe: When Jennifer was younger, she read the *Harry Potter* series three times and saw the movies over and over. When she met the *Harry Potter* star, Daniel Radcliffe, she recalls, "I screamed at him the first time that I met him."

Miley Cyrus: Jennifer went to Madonna's 2014 Oscar after-party and was very nervous. "If you get invited, you're like, you know, super-important," she said. "And I puked on [the] porch. I was in such bad condition, and I look behind me while I'm puking and Miley Cyrus is there like, 'Get it together!'"

A PRANK BACKFIRES

At a charity event, Jennifer and *Tonight Show* host Jimmy Fallon came up with a plan to dance with Jennifer Lopez. "I was like, we'll do a spin and then we'll go, 'Dance with us' [to J.Lo]. I do it, and then I look and he's gone! It's just me looking at J.Lo, going 'Dance with . . . me?' And she was just looking at me. Made me look like a freak in front of J.Lo!"

Pizza Pizza

Jennifer loves toppings like pepperoni, pineapple, onions, and peppers . . . just no sardines!

EITHER/OR

DOGS OR CATS?
Both

PUREBRED OR RESCUE?
Rescue

BIG MAC OR SUSHI?
Big Mac

PHILLY CHEESESTEAK OR FILET MIGNON?
Philly cheesesteak

CHEETOS OR CELERY?
Cheetos

LITTLE-KNOWN FACTS

- Jennifer didn't do the alert whistle in *The Hunger Games*. "Apparently I'm a bad whistler," she recalled. So they hired a whistle-over!

- Jennifer constantly snacked on Sour Patch Kids, Skittles, and jelly beans during the filming of *The Hunger Games*.

- Jennifer once said that she wanted "to bathe in a pool full of pasta" after getting her first real check.

When Jennifer cut her hair short in 2014, it caused headlines!

WILL JENNIFER'S DREAMS COME TRUE?
YES! YES! YES!

"Acting, films, scripts, [are] literally the only thing[s] I'm 100 percent confident in," Jennifer told *Elle*. "I know what I'm doing. I just understand it, and I love it. When I'm on the set, that's when I feel the most at home and in control."

Jennifer's name has been linked to at least four 2015 films. *The Hunger Games: Mockingjay—Part 2* is a definite and so is *Joy*, the real-life story of Joy Mangano, a Long Island housewife who created the Miracle Mop of TV infomercial and shopping-network fame. There are even whispers that *Joy* could result in another Oscar nomination for Jennifer!

Jennifer has a lot of respect for directors, and she has worked with the best of them. She might even want to work behind the camera someday herself. "I've always wanted to direct," Jennifer told *Vanity Fair*. "Ever since [*The Poker House*]. Lori Petty was directing, and I was imagining being a director. I love filmmaking. I love acting, but I don't feel married to being just in front of the camera."

Future Plans

"Ten years from now, I might be running a rodeo."

However, as much as she loves filmmaking, Jennifer has a personal life, too. And she told *Madame Figaro* that it will always be more important than her professional life. "I want my life as normal as possible. One of the dangers in the film industry is that things are too fast, aging . . . I do not want to burn the stages of my life."

With Jennifer's down-to-earth attitude and talent, it doesn't look as if she will be going up in flames anytime soon . . . unless it's as Katniss, Girl on Fire!

Resources

BOOKS

Allen, Audrey. *Jennifer Lawrence*. New York: Gareth Stevens Publishing, 2014.

Higgins, Nadia. *Jennifer Lawrence: The Hunger Games' Girl on Fire*. Minneapolis: Lerner Publications, 2013.

Krohn, Katherine E. *Jennifer Lawrence: Star of The Hunger Games*. Minneapolis: Lerner Publications, 2012.

Facts for Now

Visit this Scholastic Web site for more information on **Jennifer Lawrence**:
www.factsfornow.scholastic.com
Enter the keywords **Jennifer Lawrence**

Glossary

accolades *(AK-uh-laydz)* awards and honors

anxiety *(ang-ZYE-i-tee)* a feeling of worry or fear

audition *(aw-DISH-uhn)* a short performance by an actor, singer, musician, or dancer to see whether he or she is suitable for a part in a play, concert, or other performance

paparazzi *(pahp-uh-RAHT-zee)* photographers who follow celebrities and try to take photos of them in everyday situations

pilot *(PYE-luht)* a single episode of a TV show that is used to determine whether an entire series should be produced

Index

Acknowledgments

Page 7: Imagination: *Seventeen* April 2012
Page 8: Boring person: *NOW* March 29, 2013; Brothers: *InStyle* December 2012; Youngest girl: *Elle* May 2011
Page 9: "Nitro": *Madame Figaro* November 2013
Page 10: Preschool: *Rolling Stone* April 12, 2012; Changing schools: *The Sun* March 6, 2013; Weirdo: *Vogue* September 2013
Page 12: Script: *Glamour* April 2012; Jennifer Strong: IMDB
Page 14: Dr. Lawrence: *People* Special Oscar Guide 2011
Page 15: Flats: *Fabulous* March 25, 2013
Page 17: Stories: *Elle* May 2011; Brothers/Parents: *Elle* May 2011
Page 20: Pigeonholed: *TeenVogue* May 2011; *X-Men*: *TeenVogue* May 2011
Page 21: Mystique: *People* June 2011

Page 22: Mom & books: denofgeek.com March 16, 2012
Page 23: Audition: MTV News March 13, 2012; Katniss: *Seventeen* April 2012
Page 24: Katniss: *Parade* March 17, 2012
Page 25: First *Hunger Games*: *The Telegraph* December 13, 2013
Page 26: First day on set: *Seventeen* April 2012
Page 28: Rag doll: MTV News May 18, 2011
Page 29: Allergic: *USA Today* December 6, 2013
Page 30: Fat: *Bazaar* November 2013; Pizza: *Filmbiz/The Sun* March 6, 2013; Diet: *People* March 1, 2012
Page 31: Anorexic: *Seventeen* April 2013
Page 33: Katniss's best quality: *Star* November 25, 2013; Egos: *Entertainment Weekly* January 18, 2013

Page 34: Favorite day: *Entertainment Weekly* January 18, 2013; Friendships: *Marie Claire* June 2014; Learning to dance: *OK!* February 25, 2013
Page 35: Brothers: Denofgeek.us/movies March 16, 2012; Candid: *Marie Claire* June 2014; Snarky: *ABC News/Barbara Walters Presents: The 10 Most Fascinating People of 2013* December 2013
Page 37: Red carpets: *Late Show with David Letterman* March 21, 2012; Flying: *Late Night with Jimmy Fallon* March 22, 2012; Crackup: *People Hunger Games Special* March 2012; Dieting: *US Weekly* May 4, 2011
Page 39: Justin Timberlake: EOnline.com November 7, 2013

Page 40: Six Flags: *Tigerbeat* 2013; Bill Clinton: Heatworld.com November 7, 2013; Brad & Angelina: *Jimmy Kimmel Live* 2014
Page 41: Jeff Bridges: *NY Daily News* July 24, 2013; Daniel Radcliffe: *Late Night with Seth Meyers* April 21, 2014; Miley Cyrus: *Late Night with Seth Meyers* April 21, 2014
Page 42: Pranks: *The Tonight Show with Jimmy Fallon* May 15, 2014
Page 43: Whistler: MTV News March 13, 2013; Pasta bath: *Interview* April 2012
Page 44: Acting: *Elle* December 2012
Page 45: Directing: *Vanity Fair* February 2013; Normal: *Madame Figaro* November 2013; Future Plans: *Jennifer Lawrence: The Hunger Games' Girl On Fire* 2013

About the Author

Marie Morreale is the author of many official and unofficial celebrity biographies. She attended New York University as an English/creative writing major and began her writing and editorial career in New York City. As the editor of teen/music magazines *Teen Machine* and *Jam!*, she covered TV, film, and music personalities and interviewed superstars such as Michael Jackson, Britney Spears, and Justin Timberlake/'NSYNC. Morreale was also an editor/writer at Little Golden Books.

Today, she is the executive editor, Media, of Scholastic Classroom Magazines writing about pop-culture, sports, news, and special events. Morreale lives in New York City and is entertained daily by her two Maine coon cats, Cher and Sullivan.